KISMET

by Jo Patti

Kismet is published under Imagine books, sectionalized division under Di Angelo
Publications INC.

IMAGINE BOOKS

an imprint of Di Angelo Publications.Kismet. Copyright
2017 Jo Patti in digital and print distribution in the United
States of America.

Di Angelo Publications

4265 San Felipe #1100

Houston, Texas, 77027

www.diangelopublications.com

Library of congress cataloging-in-publications data

Jo Patti. *Kismet*. Downloadable via Kindle, iBooks and nook.

_____
Library of Congress Registration

Paperback

ISBN-10: 1-942549-18-0

ISBN-13: 978-1-942549-18-5

Layout: Di Angelo Publications

Cover Design: Di Angelo Publications

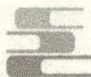

1.   Poetry 2. . Poetry —— Poetic Works——Single Authored.
      United States of America with int. Distribution.

DEDICATION

My writing is dedicated to Lauradele Patti
Munisteri Smith, my paternal aunt.   Her
love, support, inspiration, musicality and
sense of humor saved me and
strengthened me. She helped many
children and adults while she was alive.
Lauradele was not honored or
acknowledged enough during her time on
earth, yet she never seemed to mind.
This volume of verse is my belated thank
you and remembrance.

Some of these poems have previously appeared in the following journals, books and magazines:

"Pulling Weeds", "When Loss Grabs" in *The Manhattan Poetry Journal, Volumes 2,3*

"Signal at Cape Cod", "Last Day in London", "The Twilight of A Man" "For My Grandmother" and "Wyoming Sighs" in *The Poet Magazine Volumes 1,2*

"Orienteering" *Andrew Mountain Press,*" No One Dares Say It" *Voices for Peace Anthology New York Peace and Justice Center*

"For A.J.E." *Index of American Periodical Verse, 1985*

"Sisters" *Red Ink Poetry Magazine*

"Country Courtin" *Five Bells Australian Poetry, 1999*

"Bathing in the Bin" *Escaping the Yellow Wallpaper Anthology, 2002*

"Ambush" *WorldWords Anthology, New Zealand 2006*

"In Labour" and "Spoils of War" *Di-Verse-City Austin International Poetry Festival Anthologies 2005, 2016.*

WITH GRATITUDE

There are many human beings who have
helped me along my path:
My teachers and colleagues who
encouraged me to write and were rigorous
in their reviews of my work early on in my
career: Dr. John Glavin, Barbara Jones,
Kenneth D. Kelleher, (Mary) Jo
Anderson, Dr. Alan Altimont and Auntie
Beatrice Ballangarry.
Those who have passed from this Earth
but who motivated me when they were
alive and help me still: My
Grandmothers: Gertrude Inez Ziniti Patti
Munisteri and Rose Lamont Grasso.   My
friends, mentors: Valerie Mather
Wainright, Charlene Dawn Blue Horse,
Mary Brave Bird, Ms. Carol Bumpass, Dr.
Charles Socarides, Dr. Arnold Mysior, my
grandfather Peter Pino Munisteri and my
son, Denali Martin Waldemar Schmidt.

Most importantly I am grateful for my
daughter, Sequoia Patti Karanema
Schmidt who I continue to learn from and
whose expertise and creative guidance
encourages me to attempt new adventures
in life and to finally finish this book.

Table of Contents

PULLING WEEDS

I entered here these holy fields
and made a sacrilege.
I cleanse myself with Adam's curse
my needs be I must always work this is
what being cast from Paradise brings.

The self-inflicted punishments abate
with each root I heave,
persist with each I neglect.
Sun rays pound my sweating back
thwarted now and then
by elusive desert winds
cool, not cold.

I stoop, I must. It's easier, less draining
if I want to save my strength
for the next hallowed ground.
But here, at least one can see where it all
ends. Always in the periphery
border lines, barbed wire
swaying in uncertainty
readied for the next strike.

I have the chance to gasp in sunrise.
Standing here I mutter. It's beauty
is the bane of my existence, reminding me
of how many sunrises I have missed,
how many weeds clutch the soil
escaping mine,
how often I stoop, how little I stand
how terribly trivial must seem my sins.

(Israel)

SHARM EL SHEIK

Sharm El Sheik where the chic
come to swim
In the ahmar sea, the weather
always warm
Waiters wearing pendant smiles
speaking in honey tones
As the azura waters beckon
all who can see.

At the cyber café akdar and cool
I can keyboard my poems
like a shams struck fool
No one pays attention
to an elder woman alone and free.

'Mumkin-computer?' I inquire of the man
at the front desk.
He gestures without looking at me, points
to a cubicle in the back.

Too many hours in the sun
or in front of screen light
With no blinds, I am dazed by Egypt
After days of respecting Ramadan
my stomach is vocal
If I sit here all day no one minds, I am
invisible, quiet.

Ah! Sharm El Sheik, I am spellbound
by your sands and salt waters
The charm and grace of your people
promenading in the evening
the trance of the open sky.

(Egypt)

LAKOTA MAN

I would wish, I'd never walked the hills
never stood atop the bluff
gazing out over Wanblee.
I would wish I'd never returned your look
or let your arms encircle my waist
in the starlight.
I would wish I hadn't laid back
into the sweet grasses
felt your heart beating on mine or tasted
your breath.
I would wish we hadn't gone
down to the creek
where others disturbed our silence
as we listened for the drum.

I would wish some nights, that what had
been was a dream
for crossing the line between
what might be and what was
has seared my heart and branded my soul.

I would wish, Lakota man,
I could speak to someone about you
yet what would I say ? That once
there was a Lakota man
who pulled me out of time
where we crossed and defied unwritten,
rigid rules of race,
culture, country and age.

Or once, there was a Lakota man
who dared me to be with him
against the prejudice of brothers, sisters,
mothers, fathers
urging my eyes and heart open
to the compromises
I'd forced my spirit to make;
then he left me to swallow
this new found clarity in solitary
behind steel doors.

When the prison gate was opened
I did not walk home free.
Circles upon circles on the plains of 3 mile
creek and Oglala
my feet moved in a steady beat
speaking through the earth
remembering, knowing he was not far
but not knowing just how near.

I would wish some days
that I had seen him again
had pressed my forehead into his
to say goodbye.
I would wish I could have listened more
to you, Lakota man
listened with my hands, my eyes
my mouth...

But a spirit greater than each of us
has not willed this wish to be.

(South Dakota, USA)

TASTING RICE

He says
"Hey, I'll be your joy boy
your toy boy, your anytime
goodtime man.
I'm not banana ya know
like yellow on the outside
white on the inside.
I'm the tame tiger, ja shin master
Unhaired, dim sum dumpling lover man
da real ting baby...good eh?"

I trade in my Mao bow
for fancy cars, VCRs, blue-eyed girls,
western, bestest everything
cause money is freedom baby
I don't care.
I wannabe capitalist, too, like you.
You teach me, you reach me
you're West meets East
crazy Hollywood, Texan tied,
New York city woman
big American dream
in a small size package, eh?"

I say,
"Hey, what happened
to ancient Tao wisdom

slow opening lotus blossoms, silk robes,
pillow books, inscrutable looks,
bowls of rice
and wooden chopsticks?
Where are your tai chi black slippers
baggy pants, strident high pitched tones?
Let's see your whip scars
from the Red army
your thin straw mattress, painted scrolls
calligraphy brushes, butterfly harp
or lucky charms.

How come
you know more American TV programs
more brands of cars, soap,
fast food, cat food
than I do?
How come you're so tall
bold, smooth skinned, not yellow
and you can dance?
I wanted you cause
you be the mysterious orient
silent meditation, moxibustion,
fire of the dragon
Szechuan sesame noodles
all in an egg roll, mister."

We laugh together.
He says
"Boy sister, we got brainwashed good.
Let's be snakes in the sand, apple crumble
nipping dogs, lapping water,
mash potatoes,
brown rice, fried rice
basmati if you like.
We eat now, eh? Anytime."

I tell my girlfriend from Hong Kong;
"I'm seeing this Huang Yee guy,
ya know?"

She says

"Don't mind he's cruel
that's just Chinese."
I say I know what she means...eh.
She looks then laughs at me.
"Ah, so you have finally tasted rice?"

I smile inscrutably and tease
"Oh, wouldn't you like to know."

(San Jose, California, USA)

WHEN THE MEN WOULD GO

Waking up to the sound of radio Shalom
Gazing out the window
at the enveloping desert,
we're waiting
for the lumbering step of the big men
the joking and laughter of the young men,
the coughing and hacking
of the older ones...
but we heard none of these sounds
one morning.

Drawing an audible inward breath
I know in an instant of recognition
they had gone.
They had gone quickly and quietly
with secret orders,
maneuvers in the night
Forces mobilized
at all the borders simultaneously
active and reserve military called for
an exercise or a real emergency
no one knew.

We were suddenly in limbo for a time
rocking ourselves silently
I kept staring out the window
Scanning, hoping to see one we knew

but all were gone, vaporized.
Only swirling red dust
encircled the kibbutz
leaving us alone, together
when the men would go.

When the men would go
women sang louder during work time
softer around sleep time.
Fingers would drum away hours
in the evenings
children cried more than usual.
There was caution in our mouths
hope in our hearts, sorrow in our eyes.

We would breathe in resolution,
no one mentioning the obvious
as we went on working, working
all of us praying, praying for peace.

When the men had gone.
When the men would go.

(Sinai, Israel)

GAWKING AT BADDE MANORS

Sydney sider, high heeled smooth walker
crossing between traffics lights
just hopping, bopping up to the footpath
as she slides her cellular phone
from her hip pocket to her right cheek
pausing to remember a coded number
pressing, caressing buttons
as she's struttin
sassy repartee all the way
to the roundabout.

Will ya, won't ya look up at me?
Don't you see the storm coming, baby?

Now halt for a nanosecond, darlin.
I am eyein, spying you,
you beauty in a three-pieced suit.
Who are you speaking to?

I wanna come outta that line
like a swift-tongued viper
shock you, block you, bite your tongue
till you dance into oblivion.

Drop that damn funny phone
Take off your glasses, honey.
Swing your briefcase in swollen spirals.

Kick off your spike shoes to the sun,
sugar-then both of us
yowl down on the concrete
whadaya say?

(Sydney, Australia)

GANGGAALI

Dedicated to Colleen Walker, missing
since 1990, and to the memory of Evelyn
and Clinton murdered in Bowraville, NSW
in 1990-1991.

All the welled up sobs in silence
All the uncried tears in men
All the sweat from centuries of labour
Make the rivers run again.

Ganggaali, ganggaali
The sky is crying, crying
Crying for Colleen.

And the earth is soaked in sorrow
And her mother's eyes are red
And the color blind in Bowra
Close their mouths and bow their heads.

Ganggaali, ganggaali
Power in the rainstorm
Keening for Colleen.

So the wind roars like the ocean
As she calls for help in dreams
As her clothes float down the river
Her body never seen.

The streets and churches empty
The courthouse drenched in shame
The children wake from nightmares
Afraid to say her name.

Ganggaali, ganggaali, ganggaali
Our throats are parched and hoarse
From shouting for Colleen.

Although the search is over
Two more crosses on the hill
The third to add to thousands
We're unsure of even still.

Ganggaali,ganggaali
Where is our tender daughter?
Has yet another child been slaughtered?
Call out now for Colleen.

End the agony of not knowing
Recall her face, recall that night
There is a mercy found in truth
Healing wounds for black and white.

Ganggaali, ganggaali
Let the children in Bowra be.
Will no one please come forward
Release the spirit of Colleen?

Ganggaali, ganggaali
Ganggaali, ganggaali
    Ganggaali.

*Ganggaali means 'to call out' in the Gumbaynggir language

(NSW, Australia)

INVISIBLE MEN

Whatever you do, don't
go hunting in Transylvania
for a lover, darling.

Take a good look first.
Verify your own humanity
by bringing a pocket mirror.
See the echo of your visage
make sure he's got one, too.
They say, like attracts like
the void sucks out life.

Whatever you do, don't
be sleeping alone
in Transylvania, dear.

Put a crucifix by your pillow
let a dog sleep by your bed.
Close the curtains, bolt the door.
Tune in to Christian music
on your radio. They say
you never can be too careful.

Don't ya know, darlin
when the time comes
you'll have to have the courage
to drive a stake into his heart
slicing off his head

severing all connection
to the darkness
that infects your love.

So, whatever you do, don't
go dancing in the moonlight
in Transylvania, honey.

Save your howls
with your garlic
for daytime...by the ocean.

(Austin, Texas USA)

LAST DAY IN LONDON

In a bath
not a Roman one
he's slid languid
against the tiles.
Smoking a cigarette
over the edge
his other arm
careless on the tub
as if he's in his old armchair
or on an accustomed throne,
he flicks ashes on to wet linoleum
his head still propped
against the tiles.

His lips pout smoke
then closing, swim in menthol.
His lips rimmed red
as if he's just made love.
His eyes are liquid
his lashes dark with waters
his pupils steamed and widened
from the bath.

He swallows thoughts
his throat dry, dripping
the indent of his neck
I'd want to touch
he wants to wash.

The water tries a tiny tide
it ebbs his nipples
dark now, pert.
The hairs on his navel float
like filamentous brown seaweed
his body hairs undulate
deep to the sides.

He languishes warms
his feet touching the taps
his toes grasping cool aluminum
his buttocks squeaking as he
slides on the white porcelain
echoing under the water.

Steam rolls from the bath
like fog off a seashore
he listen for horns
he listens for more.
He shifts and his pores
suck warm water his cigarette
drops to the floor.

He gropes for blue towels
the water line lowered
he leans over dousing
his life in the cigarette
he stands naked, streaming
believing he is clean.

INCLEMENT RENDEVOUS

Like a jungle sky
before the lightening rips
and rains bow the giant ferns
wash the leopards spots
polish the armor of rhinoceros beetles;
I think of you tumultuously
 in broad blur strokes:
blues, silver-white, smoke, blacks and grey
soon to follow, altering the calm
and ominous beauty of this landscape
by a crack in the clouds pouting thunder
because there are storms
whenever we meet.

Whether you be on land
or aboard a steamer bound for Calais
whether I be on the adjacent pillow
or continents away
we brew in dreams
our subconscious climates
sharing currents that defy boundaries
or meteorology
we create new atmospheres.

Perhaps you harbor a secret grudge
from a former life
and thoroughly drenched
in a lover's amnesia

we stumble into each other
entwined around our mutual past
like lianas on bulwark trunks
centuries old.

Have I put rings around your core a
sampling of which would show
a decade of violent weather...

(Belize)

MINUET

I.   Petals
        cerise petals
        draped on still water
        floating in a green crystal bowl
        pristine

II.   Grandma
        comes on tiptoe
        blows gently, leans forward
        the cerise petals glide, lilt, furl
        travel

III.   Grandma
        seeing all this
        remembers her homeland
        quiet, Spring, canals, gondolas
        Venice

IV.   Music
        from a distant
        radio fills her ears
        finds her feet and fingers moving
        dancing

V.   Rapture
        from Caruso's
        voice, causes her to hum
        then sing in chorus with dancing
        dreaming

VI.   As she
        sways and full turns
        oblivious, she reels
        banging the wooden table with
        a start

VII.   Aghast
        she stops saddened
        by the sight of her bowl
        overturned, petals bruised, water
        dripping.

(Brooklyn, New York)

ORIENTEERING

With the curtains closed
I could be
anywhere.

With my eyelids closed
you could be
anyone.

Every time I shut my sight
every time I pull in tight
one touch, one odor
drives me back,
steers me clear of revelry
parks me into privacy
sparks a fuse
of intimate please
for me, for you, for more
connections.

Tooting my nose
after tears
rambling prose
rambling fears,
little windshield wipers
wash your tongue
before your words
get dirty.

Your sleeves are rolled up
all air tight
you make a fist
but not to fight.
You clench a pen
but not to write.

The motor keeps on running
you turn it over
under my skin
I don't want to lose
but I don't care to win.

How far can you crawl
under the covers
without getting lost
or missing your mother.

We have the directions
just not the time
chosen destinations
yet can't read the signs.

(Sussex, England)

34

SIGNAL AT CAPE COD

Up and out of the motel room
dawn rising
(at ten some degree of independence)
skipping in the sand
singing with the ups and downs
waves receding in low tide
feeling like a young gull flying
for the first time.

My hands flapping
my legs longer than I'm quite used to
breezes against my orange shirt
my budding breasts.

No one to caution me from leaping
no voice to chastise me
for "unladylike" behavior
I shout on the wind
open my mouth like a hungry fish
for the sea spray,
when my foot is startled
by a queer sensation.

I look down, gaping at a washed up
shark's head
I have found him on this beach
my morning mood alters.

Crouching down, curious
I look at his unseeing eye
ragged flesh cut off about the neck.
I jump up and down
in impromptu Indian dances.

My father must have heard me, or maybe
he, too, wants to be on the sands
the last morning in Cape Cod.
Anyway, he sees me
I run to him, pull him over
to appraise my 'catch'.

His ten year old delight bursts through
quickly he is kneeling, examining
the specimen.
He pronounces what I already know, that
I "have found a shark's head!"

My father tells me to wait right there.
Obediently, I guard my prize
while watching the gulls
circling overhead.

My father returns with his movie machine.
Instructing me to repeat all my actions
exactly as if it were the first time
I encounter the creature.

Directions I take well.
We film it on the first try
my father is pleased.

He tells me some peoples
would consider this an augury
an auspicious sign that something
is about to change in their life.

I look at him filming the beach
this last summer we
will be on the east coast
and I secretly hope
that this time, he is telling the truth.

(Cape Cod, Massachusetts, USA)

EXCURSIONS

I drifted and woke
to the sound of rain
like cellophane crumpled
on my window, it runs down.

I rise and part shower curtains
feeling for the faucets
hot, then cold, as water streams
in ping, pang, ching
eastern melodies on porcelain
water over my eyelids
washing my lashes
like a gentle fire hosing
my body is awoken.

Drip, echo, pat
the faucet holds out on me
lending a last drop
as I squeeze my hair
dry my feet thinking:

"Over the bridge
over the bridge
over the bridge, I walked
    the Piazza Liberta.

Down the steps
down the steps
down the steps I went
making sounds like a tin pan clanging
    the Piazza Liberta.

Past the whistles
past the stares
shielding the glare with green sunglasses
    the Piazza Liberta.

Ah, Ah...Italy!"

(Florence, Italy)

FOR MY GRANDMOTHER

Now we know it will come
I pray it comes quickly.
Now they fear it will come
they watch and they wait
not patiently like you,
but with present frenzy
for past neglect
for passed opportunities
for future guilt.

What must you see?
Eyes still glazed with regret
mouths set with resolutions
hands facile from use
ears sharpened by practice
in the classroom, in the kitchen
in the garden, in the bedrooms.

Your head tilts to one side
your hair soft, white and fine.
Without glasses, you focus on the paths
of least resistance, too tired to explore
as you once did.

You must see everything.
Clever, even now
you filter out whisperings
and condescension.

For their benefit.
You humor them by smiling, taking pills
you know will only stall
your sought for peace
your seeking silence.

We walk around the block
for my sake.
You cry on my shoulder
about my 'real' grandfather
about your first love, your lost love
and I cry for mine, and for you.

You know
You know it will come
ease you out of life
out of my life.

Yet I, too pray
it comes quickly.
For by now
you have forgotten
your prayers.

(New York City, USA)

TO MY SON AS HE TURNS SEVEN

Before you came to us
I saw you
whole and naked, lifted up
crying healthily for me.

I was surrounded
by beautiful, brave women
sage smoke, prayers, chants in a circle
of love, courage and mystery.
I had to eat my fear
face my demons, die awhile
before you could come.

Before you came to us
I stood in the bright lights
danced on ramps, whirled in the shadows
climbed desert mountains
dove in the ocean
froze in mountain lakes
basked naked in the sun
I was almost full with life
before you came.

And when you entered
a flash of white light
under an Indian blanket
your father panting
me smiling all over
the sun at mid-day or near it
the sound of the ocean outside,
music and young men laughing below us.
I held my breath I wanted you so
when you did come to us.

While you were inside of me
I saw with new eyes,
my senses gifted with you
my belly swelling with you
your name came readily then
many moons before you were born.

While we were one flesh
you kicked, rolled and hiccoughed inside.
I spoke and sang to you
before you came to us,
we were alone waiting
for your father to join us.

And when you came to us
after days of sweat, water and walking,
you were as I had seen you
only more beauteous, with open eyes
not crying, whole and healthy.

Your father, not I, held you first.
I was in a sleep
my eyes could not see you
but I felt the cord cut
and inner joy rushed to my arms
to hold you.

My eyes spilled with gratitude
my heart with love
as they do still
now you are here with us.

(Bundilla, NSW, Australia)

ECHO

What is it?
He neither looks, nor smells, nor speaks
like this boy I remember.
Now, in early winter
I recall a humid summer night
sitting in the front seat
each of us languishing
against opposing doors
silent, uncertain,
we are lit by a street lamp.

We have touched
we have parted.
I was satisfied
he, unrequited.

Why is it?
I slide my hand over this back.
Flash...I return thirteen years
to the heat, to a sorrow so careless.
These ribs of my husband
must ripple this memory to the surface.

I am moaning.
My back cracks suddenly
releasing this tension I didn't realize.

My husband's chest is still a boy's chest
I bury my head.
See, I bury my head.
I can't bury my heart.

(Santa Cruz, California, USA)

MABEL'S TEARS

Inspired by the stories told to me by Neville
Buchanan about his life as an aboriginal man
of the Gumbaynggirr people

Sun was rising in the sky
with steady, stately grace.
Little girl was looking up
with wonder on her face.
Kookaburras laughed and screeched
a warning to the child.
She turned around in time to see
her father going wild.

She heard the sound of horses then,
hearts galloping with fear.
Her family rushing round the camp,
her uncles running, singin out
"Welfare cumin, welfare cumin,
the Welfare cumin here."

Older children dashed ahead
they knew where they could hide.
Their cousins and their aunties
running by their side.

Fathers stood outside their huts
defending in silent rage,
mothers holding babies
intertwined in a fierce embrace.

The little girl was frozen
her limbs paralyzed by fear.
Her mother braved the officers
to hold her daughter near.

But the horses circled round her
men dismounted with no shame
as they tore her from her child's arms
she wailed her daughter's name.

"Mabel. Don't take my Mabel!"
Her voice breaking with the pain.

They shoved Mabel in a sulky
with the other 'coloured' kids.
She searched the crowd
for her mother's face
She saw her uncle try to chase
but the welfare galloped
at a terrible pace
too soon they were far away.

Little prisoners
carted off
far, far away.

Mabel was shy of seven
when she was made into a slave.

Up at dawn
only milk to eat
doing domestic chores.
Bed at night
but little sleep
as she cried, sleeping on the floor.

Mabel nursed one dream
through the days and nights
(besides to run away).
She vowed when she had her children
no "welfare" would take them away.

She made up funny songs in her head
hum them working, all day long.
They'd protect her
from feeling the beatings
and the ache of her family...gone.

Till at last the day
when she came of age
she slipped out after dark one night
she walked back to find her family
she walked with all her might.

But as she came to her own home place
nothing was the same.
The bark huts and open fires were gone
all her family had been moved on
forced out as the white fellas came.

She kept walking by the sea
diggin pipis in the sand.
After a while she stopped to rest
she felt good there, on that land.

It wasn't long thereafter
she met a 'tiger' of a man.

His walk was steady, stately
his eyes were warm like fire.
His muscles were strong
his heart was kind
she felt with him
that she would find
a good father for her child.

They had to live on the mission
both working far from home.
Mabel taking care of white women's kids
till she had children of her own.

Her sons came first
with their father's eyes
the house was full of joy.
She sang while sweeping, cooking
"I'll always be here for you, my boys."

Then came her little daughters
and more sons till their house was full.
Yet her own parents, she never found
her own tribe, she never knew.

Mabel would wake before sunrise
listening for the welfare car.
If she heard it come
she'd grab her sons
in the black berry bushes
they'd hide.

Behind the blood gum
she placed her daughters
her husband, ready inside.

But the welfare car
just passed them by
went on to another home.
Mabel and Tiger seemed to be safe
'protection board'
left their mob alone.

Then one Saturday early
after yarnin all Friday night,
Mabel, Tiger and the children
slept in past the dawn's first light.

She heard the car doors shut outside
she felt the cold about
she saw the white men enter
no time to rise and shout.

She clutched her youngest to her
her boys were handcuffed, led away
They shoved Tiger hard against the wall
all she could do was pray.

She ran outside
in time to watch
as they slammed the door to go.
Tears were streaming
down to her breasts
her children
were hers
no more.

Mabel stumbled back with her baby
Tiger sighed as he reached for his son.
No more of what happened
could be talked of
No more could be said, or done.

The word was put round
bout their children
Tiger saw them in the fire some nights.
Mabel kept in her heart her precious five
She never gave up her fight.

Years passed, they had more young ones.
Mabel taught them to hide in the back.
Welfare took other children away
But Mabel kept them off her track.

Till one evening as Mabel was sweeping
and singing a funny song
she heard that car drive up the road
she smelt there was something wrong.

Tiger was still out working
she grabbed her children, quick.
She ran to hide them out the back
but she stumbled over a stick.

The welfare sent three men this time
they surrounded Mabel's kids
they told her to go and get them
their clothes
But it all was a terrible trick.

(Bowraville, NSW, Australia)

GIVE US A KISS

Nicotine, lipstick and liquor
with breath
that would knock you over
she insists
that I kiss her.

There's no way out
her fleshy lips expectant
I oblige.
I kiss her
like I kissed frogs when I was little
to prove to my brothers
I wasn't afraid.

I kiss her
with my nose pinched
my toes clenched
my arms by my ribcage.
I kiss her
as she's grinning
as she's winning
as I wince.

I kiss her
to quiet her, to shut her up
to pacify.

She lets me go
then sneaky like a serpent
she bites me from behind
plants a print
on my neck
as her lips press, then leave me.

I stand there unwilling
to be ever kissed by her
again.

(Houston, Texas, USA)

THE BOY WITH THE BUTTERFLY KNIFE

He tells me the reason he hangs around
this particular bar
is cause he loves the music
on their juke box
not especially the clientele. I serve him
another beer
listening as he winds down
by spurting his Aussie tales.
It's late. Sometimes my mind flickers
to the other end of the counter.
Can't help it.
Then he ejaculates his long 'a's'
so instantly
I pay attention.
His knows his enchantments
work on 'Amariken' girls.

I don't understand it, really the music
is from twenty years ago,
bout the time I figure he was born.
He says he imagines
the 60's were the best time to be
in the U.S.A.
I take down another order.

Someone accidentally shoves me.
The Aussie
doesn't grasp New York protocol
he turns too sharply
becomes all fire. I touch his shoulder
we see each other clear.
I feel grateful when he takes
a sip of beer real slow
nods in my direction. I have to pass him
on the way to serve my other customers.

He tags me on my return.
"Don't worry, possum," he smiles, leaning
down to unroll his left sock.
I detect a glint in those eyes
and hurry to the kitchen.

When he signals me again
there is a butterfly knife out defiantly
on the bar.
He is tapping his feet
to the Rolling Stones
bobbing his chin, grinning straight to me.
My look is steady. "Very handy,"
I whisper,
"Very illegal." He takes this
for a come on.
He sits up straight so I can see his chest
I still see a boy.
"Last call" is shouted through the smoke.
Elvis keeps on singing
through the juke box.

Both of us are reeking of beer.
His mouth, my hands
our shirts. He circles his head
then teases me
as I wipe the counter clean.

"You need a vacation, that's what."
"Sure do." I sigh.
"So, if ya can't get to Australia,
bring a little of Australia ta you."
"A little?" I sass. He does
make me giggle.
Can't help it, but I worry about that
butterfly knife.

He tries to nudge me in the ribs
"Ya aren't from the city are ya?"
The lights open up on our faces.
I confess my Texas ties.
The Aussie licks his lower lip.

Tips could have been better
If I'd paid more attention
to my other tables.
I shrug it off as I count the change
and single bills.

This Aussie is bold. He sends a charge
from that smiling face
and broad hairless chest.

I'm thinking, in spite of those green eyes,
he'll have to drop that butterfly knife
before I tell him my name.

"Hey, Jessie..." my boss yells.
The Aussie winks at me.
"My name is Jack. Plain, but true."
I believe him.
He puts a fiver down as peace offering.
I put up my apron.
He slides off the stool saying,
"Mind if I see ya home?
I could do with company for a walk."

He puts one foot in front of another with
ease a country strider.
He makes me laugh some more.
I forget we are surrounded by concrete.
But I remember that butterfly knife
strapped to his shin.

We approach the doorway to my building.

"Listen," I fib, "I'm married."
The Aussie stops. "Lucky fella" he says,
smashing his hands into his pockets.
I sit in the stairwell till I'm sure he is gone.
To me, the cars rushing by
sound like waves.
I dream all night of tropical birds,
islands in the Pacific.

NO ONE DARES SAY IT

On a bench
in a transport station
sitting
for buses, trains or
subways.

In an ordinary setting
supermarkets, the neighborhood park
amidst laughter in a restaurant
we can hear it.

No one will say it
everyone thinks it
women will whisper
men change the subject,
yet somehow we know
the readiness for war.

Not by remodeled recruiting centers
council halls or bulletins from
Washington, D.C.
Threads of laser-like warnings
nanosecond flashes we
cock to one side
huff away hoping
in unsung psalms
this decade will be different.

Moving without motion
in a march without order
to a tune we hum
we whistle in winter
the message transmitted
re-directed smiles
we smell, we dream we
premonition loneliness.

(Washington DC, USA)

WHEN MEN CRY

The time comes inevitably
a part of me waits
for their heads to drop
over my shoulder
their arms to clutch my
lower ribs
their eyes to turn
from mine.

They all eventually bury
their faces in my neck
squeeze my breath
from me
then release their sorrow
in a choked, gasping cry
as I soothe
their heaving backs.

I don't have to view
the distress
in their foreheads
or watch
their chins tremble
recoiling at their own lack
of inflicted self-controls.

I know the landscape of
their bodies
from the palms
of my hands.

The splinters of their pain
will take me a long while
to extract
their catharsis leaving
a bitter taste in my mouth
as I drink
and swallow my pride
again and again.

I suppose
I should be grateful
when they end by
forgiving me
peer hopefully
into my eyes
for renewed bouts.

Yet if I do not coddle
them with my smiles
massage their aching
hubris
they narrow their intimacy
or clear their throats
for future prey.

So I continue
to mime understanding
grate my emotions
against the wall
of their desires
as I fold up my needs
give others my attention
and late at night
as they fall exhausted
I rock and rub
my own silent
heaving back.

(Planet Earth)

PORT OF CALL

Where once we lingered by the docks
in doorways waiting for the ships
to lumber in by night, by dawn;
where once we shied,
shoulders up, hoping
for their swift advances, longing
for a pat on the head, a lift of our chins
a caress of our hair;
where once we sighed
we wept as they turned
to travel on and on and on...
now, we no longer heave
as they push off from their piers.

Now we give them sliver grins
only moan inside, wave our hands
let go their fingers.

Now, we stalk restlessly
on the streets, through the alleys, wary
watching the young ones,
sad for the old ones,
but tired of waiting
for our sailors to return.

We seek new faces on incoming vessels
our heads no longer turned
by blue tattoos
or whistling pirates.

Now we seek them out, direct our eyes
roll our shoulders saying;
"Come, come sailor boys,
we'll be your guides.
This is your port of call.
Call us some more.
We'll call you no more."

We take them, slip our words
between their longing
drink their beer, hold their glasses
we toast 'tonight'
for 'tonight' is the only night we have
to touch, to smell, to sail
into the port of call.
Tonight, they'll batter us down
in rafter beds
we'll taste their sea salt skin
remind them of colleens, summer corn,
former first loves
and home...they've come home.
And tonight, we'll almost believe
they have come home, yes
they've come home.

The tide is going out
they know it keen, that sense of time
shifting off us
out of sleep as sirens blow
their boots go on
our charm ebbs out their eyes
splashing warm into last kisses
receding in a mirror as we watch them
take their leave, take
take their leave, take, take
their leave.

(Morocco)

WHEN LOSS GRABS

When loss grabs
and stays unwilling
Clutching with meat hooks
at my feet
I slide
out of my skin
raw and tender
then lie on the floor
prostrate and broken
pleading with the tiles
to help me
let go.

When loss licks
with viperous tongues
pleasure buds poisoned
with its black humors,
the void from freedoms
sucked in greed
leaves me crawling thirsty
facing a wall.

When loss slaps
with bullwhip cracks
beating my eyes
with ammonia memories,
I limp to the bed
in violent heaves
gripping the spread
with metallic fingers
my tired trembling talon hand
slips in then out
with the razor blade.

As life drips out
then loss lets go.

(New York City, USA)

SISTERS

Hawk, I see you there
huddled in the corner
claws on concrete
waiting in the warehouse on the rez
like me: caught
wings clipped, watching
with a wary eye.

As we approach you blink
but do not look away as we step near you.
Why are you here?
Will they make fans
of your splendid wings?
Stuff your noble head
clip and dry your claws for remembrance
of your own swift sweeps for tucker?

No more will you fly sister
yet you do not shudder.
I can see your breath expand
your lower body
even now a steady rhythm
through your bones.

Never will I forget your stare
or being so close to you
for you were the first I beheld
eye to eye on the ground.

Like you, I wanted to fly away that day
away to Denver and out to the coast
over the Pacific and back to my children.
My wings were broken, too.

Maybe you also miss your children
at least I can still see, write, hop around;
you friend are dismembered by now
feathers pulled and scattered.
Who has pieces of you, sister?

Your eye follows in me still
by and by I will be with you in the skies
above we will fly, looking down below
free sister, free again.

(Rosebud, South Dakota, USA)

BATHING IN THE BIN

Unconsciously a libation
I poured water over my shoulders
while sitting in a porcelain tub.
Nurses knelt beside me
an orderly held a clipboard
bright lights shot through me
I was illuminated for their benefit
Every mark, every scar
every unusual feature
noted meticulously by men with pens
couldn't they wait?
Was I to be some fish bait
dangled on a hook for bigger prey
attractive as long as I was squirming
flapping as I was cast out, electrified
my agonies as a lure to reel in others.

I splashed the water with my flipper feet
eyes crawling all over me
big men, white and black, gaped
I was naked.

Couldn't they finish?
An undercurrent of voices
chanting possible medications,
Thorazine, Stelazine, Haldol
Librium, Lithium, Zoloft

I am never consulted
but keep laughing absurdly
as they roll me over
stabbing my back with stares
poking me with callous fingertips
the water is getting tepid
my flesh raises from the chill.

They tell me not to wash my hair
I stand robotically waiting for towels.
My flank is pinched before I receive them.

I keep smiling to the end
No one seems to get the joke.

(Texas, USA)

THE SECRET GAMES

Those cruel violations
those cursed progenitors
perverted, pre-occupied
undone by their own fantasies
fingers touching forbidden zones
"Don't touch me, please don't touch me!"
Mercilessly they toy and play
on their own flesh and blood,
extracting oaths, swearing secrets
assured of servile silence
obedience to their whims insured,
they twist and writhe in their own desires
coerce us into games
then make us out as liars,
beat their offspring into putty
psyches scared beyond their years.

A sorrow so deep.
A shame so hidden,
only decades of love convince them
to confide their fears
their terror of closets, basements,
dark places,
bedrooms, bathrooms, attic spaces.
Will no one believe that their mother
or uncle or father or neighbor
inflicted this torture
beyond physical nature,

wracked their erogeny, thwarted sexuality
forcing them to carry this terrible secret
to bed with their lover, their husband
another who'll cleanse them of memory
without stain or defilement.

Erase what can never be written
offer no bribes, inflict no punishments.

Those cruel violations, cursed progenitors.
Cruel violators. Curse those progenitors.

(Washington DC)

WYOMING SIGHS

Sitting in the back seat
contorting in efforts to sleep
the warmth from a body on my lap
the wind trying to lash in through
the rear window
choke me with chills.

His head turns on my thigh
reminding me of another's
he is riding up front now
steering the wheel
but it is me who is the driven one.

I stare out.
Clouds laden with rain and mist
sag to the open ranges, like figures
who moved when a photo
as being snapped;
miles of posts, wires, rundown windmills
blur behind us, whipped away.

No cattle for hours
they, unlike we, must have found
a secret shelter.
We are in a storm in grey,
gripping twilight.
A flat top mountain pushes skyward
bulky and striated with Wyoming earth.

We're weary of ploughing into each other
wrestling for fun
with each other's Achilles.
We'll never make the rodeo now so we
surround ourselves with music, smoke
rocking into sleep.

Up front they roll down a window.
I am opening doors faster
than I thought I could turn the knobs
but they tap in another J and don't hear
He's driving like a maverick,
galloping over roads
before it grows dark and we cross
the lines to Utah.

He's a fancy dancer; he turns
and turns my head.
But I am with his brother and it will take
more than Wyoming, the Dakotas and
Minnesota, to change that.

(Laramie, Wyoming)

77

THE TWILIGHT OF A MAN
For my father

I did not know him in his youth
nor do I really know him now.
But perhaps his smile was not so painful
then, perhaps his hands relaxed then
by his sides.

His eyes, they must have sparkled then
they do just sometimes now.
His shoulders now so dutifully held
must once have burst forth eagerly
from a prouder chest.

I suppose his gait, his manners
years before were brazen
where now he walks wary, tentative
and tired.

I guess he feels his life has passed him
like clouds at sunset chased from sight.
He supposes he'll no longer roar in
command or laughter
forget his pains, leap in joy.

He is near the end of daylight
but not the end of day.
His nights could be the happiest times
of his life. He once thought
they would be.

(Houston, Texas)

THE ENCHANTED

Like a swimmer tempts a stormy sea,
thinking
"I can push these currents through
with my able fingers, my practiced legs.
I can forge my head
into the grain of the ocean
as I have done so many times before."

As he puffs himself like a blowfish
stretching his ribcage
with deep male breaths
shaking his feet loose on the beach
his hands ready by his sides,
he spies a black flag.

The sight stings his vision, causes him
to cough the salt, grey air, then lick his lips
a reassuring gesture
before snapping his trunks
and striding to the grasping waves
sliding from the pebble beach,
sizzling as they recede
beckoning him forth to their wry
chilling embraces.

He braces himself with a slap
on his muscular thighs
a pat on his thickened buttocks,
his eyes slip to the sides of their sockets
thrusting his attention back
to the black flag,
waving and warning,
the whipped cloth ominous
threatening him to swim at his own risk
in his own folly, at no man's mercy
but the sea's.

He directs his eyes to center,
mocking the ocean with a dive
forward, his feet kicking the foam
into the mist.
He shivers with each stroke
spits out brine, petty fears
then bobs into the turgid
waters...unheeding.

He wakes, startled out of slumber
runs his hands over his face
to whip off a dream.
He shivers with a cigarette
the alarm giving him hours
before the official day
he curses his vow and yearns for a fix.

He manages a walk to the bathroom
down the hall
turns on the taps, stands somnolent

for warm water.
A splash lets him remember with
uncomfortable alacrity
the too frequent nights of stains
on the porcelain
of kneeling to it's throne
in spasms and groaning
vomiting in cycles, a purging so violent
for a few seconds afterward he was lifted
like a helium balloon,
only to be sent crashing back to the earth
doused with cold water.

But as he emerges
he is clutched from under
with a leash wrapping him
in a rushing grip
holding him with its suction
commanding him to stay.
He tries to tread the eddies
but is washed with trepidation
with the fury of the under tides
flogging him
flailing him at their whim
 in his helplessness
he prays. He prays from fright.

Gulping in water,
he spouts furious oaths, confessions.
He cries like the gulls who circle him,
descending, scanning the sea
around him for more suitable prey.

He slaps at the ocean,
splashing his nether hopes.
He writhes in exhaustion, turns
floats on his back.

He swishes the cotton out of his mouth
with a swig and a shrug off
the night before.
He brushes his sensitive teeth
spits down the drain,
manages the walk back to his cold room.
He stares peevishly at the alarm clock and
an empty pack of menthols.

Like a hummingbird in a cramped cage,
his need torments him
ten thousand times per second.
His peristalsis pulsing
at a perilous rate.
His head burns from last night.
He wants to cool it down
just for the morning.
He hasn't a spoon or a clean line of steam.

He slinks off the bed,
his sheets sticky, salty.
He looks in the mirror
sees his drained face.

He squints and his eyes view
the desolate seawall
undesperate figures
and the waving black flag.
He feels for his legs, but a pull
on his ankles drags
him down like the Titanic
moaning and doomed
straining to send out the final S.O.S.

He takes the telephone off the hook
switches on loud, grinding rock and roll
gropes under the bed
where he stashed his gear from last night,
pleading, justifying
"One more time won't hurt me. Get me
through this day.
Just till tomorrow, that's all."
He fights an unseen fist
doubling him in the gut.
He tries to shrug it off,
then like an insect, returns to his mission
retrieves a black bag, scoops it up
onto the bed.

As he tears the cellophane with his teeth,
his bite tastes the thin paper
sending a sensory warning he discards.
Taping the syringe clear, he binds his arm
with brown tubing as he tightens his grip,
bulging veins, bursting sigh.

He sees a flash, a swimmer who's
drowning.
He counts to three as the needle
shoves into mid-vein
pins of liquid pleasure soften his hand.

But as he surrenders,
his head creating whirlpools,
he knows who defies the black flag
who battles windmills
like a jaded Don Quixote,
who swims in hurricanes,
tempts stormy seas, irreverent.
He wants more.

Foraging for sweet jane on the spur
of a nightmare
he reins in his other arm.
He leans back on moist sheets
as he unties.
He strokes his hair with his fingers,
drops the syringe, thinking
"This is best. This is better."
Rushes flying through him
like white crystal lasers.
  "I am strong. I am stronger."
He feels, thrashing in quantums
he labels, 'ecstasy'.

But his eyes, they won't obey,
focus, permit him
to see past his doorway.

He hangs out his tongue
like a dog without water.
His eyes swimming.
He bobbing into nausea.
His synapses swirling,
signaling, "Out of control"

He feels cold,
wants to feel colder.
Strips off his garments
falls onto the linoleum
breast strokes to the telephone.

He can't find the dial. Can't hear the tone.
He sinks, streaming sweat
blurred visions,
swallows his last air, folds under an ocean
he tempted in a storm.

He's sick and the last sight
is a black flag waving in a wind
whipping past him.
He cherishes his last night.
Cries wanting more.

It is the other current, sucking him down,
pulling him under.
He can fight, but not feel it. He can taste,
but not see it.
He is traveling down,
down without release.
He won't repent. He can't repeat.

His stomach is in a vice, his neck in a vice,
a terrible trap.

He swam against the grain
due warnings unheeded.
He holds up three fingers,
but no one is there,
no miracle rescue, no Hollywood endings.

The black flag is fading, shoreline receding
out of sight
there is no going back.

(Edinburgh, Scotland)

TALK, TALK

Thaw, thaw you iceberg in my chest
drip into the boiling point below my heart
turnover this humdrum
conundrum beating
melt into titter tatters please, please, please
ominous necessities haunting
my breakfast tea
I can see them there,
in the bottom of my cup
don't tell me it ain't so, so there
I know it's gonna infect me
with the sleeping sickness
awaken tumultuous seas
below an ocean of indifference
stirred after decades by a rainy Tuesday
tidal waves in my pupils washed away
by tap water
wafer thin, I'm bending over heaving
last night's din din
glad I didn't touch those desserts either.

Only an hour till lunchtime,
you woke me so late
you, yes, yes you, where the hell
are ya goin now?

Wow, one little shriek and my ears vibrate
semi-circular canals ebb and flow
over to my temples
pulsing vitriol from nothing whatsoever
to do with this
particular argument, kiddo
but never mind, I never do.

Wrap a towel around my throbbing head
and gimme whatever dose you got
mister, cuz today's gonna be
one of those days,
damn, faucet is leaking at a tortuous pace
drips taunt me as I race to the telephone,
it rings, I run.

'Hello, ...hello?" It's he, the super
man from the rat patrol
come to fix them vermin for good,
goodie, gee thanx, can't say no
more...hang up, hang up,
wrap the cord around my throat...pull
hard to cut off my circulation...
'Hey, I'm outta circulation...unwind again,
see the color rushing to my face.
A knock, knock who's there?
Another delivery
it's way past Christmas, aw swell a parcel,
brown paper package,
rip it to shreds with my nails
and a carving knife.

Little murders solve the crime. All the
rage explodes as I break these strings,
single threads, no connections
here's a goldmine, my belongings
from another era.
Do these things
belong to me; a me I no longer am,
they fool around following me
no matter where.
Maybe shedding my history
is harder than creating one.

Stash this trash, move onto the machine
waiting for me, silent in the ante room,
start the motor, then start the motor, shift
gears horizontal to vertical
dizziness stuns me
into clairvoyance for thirty seconds
till I commence
building this barrier
between me and the rest.

(New York City, USA)

LIONS COMING
THROUGH THE GATE

Light from the afternoon sun shines on
the inner arches
blackened tufa contrasting with the golden
manes of the lions
striding through the gateless entrance to
this ancient city.
Silent in the snow, glaring righteously at
the pollution
rubbish strewn from careless revels
they nod before prowling stately.

But I see them in my dreams, in artist
sketches, in tattoo parlors
In national emblems, now they are before
me here in Hayastan

Yerevan, in winter where a young child is
pulling on his grandmother's hand
pointing and laughing at their
manifestation and majesty
to most they are invisible.
She does not see them in attendance so
she scolds her grandson
for hindering her on the walk to the
markets on the freezing streets.
He tags along reluctantly. I smile at him
as he glances back.

The pride circles in the square of the
Republic glowering ominously
before apparating into the grey mist.
Taxis and marshukas slush by us, horns
honk unaware of the lions
coming through the gate.

(Yerevan, Armenia)

UNLIKELY SYMBIOSIS

You are a snake coiled inside my heart
silent, never blinking
is this love or just familiar constriction.

You move, I writhe in sympathy
my blood washing over you
my pulse throbbing with you
my aorta squeezed by you.

I inhale in heaves, wondering
is this love or just suffocation?

If I could pull you out slowly
would my renewed circulation
overwhelm me with freedom
rush through my ventricles, my auricles
cause the blood to thunder in my ears
my heart to beat so strongly
my feet could leave the ground.

Is this love or simply vertigo?
If we don't separate, I will never know.

(NSW, Australia)

SLOW ELK BLUES

Written on the Pine Ridge Reservation,
South Dakota, USA. The Lakota
people call cows--'slow Elk'

Why are cows eyes so soulful,
melancholic as they graze?
Why do they look away from the sun
when a human steps
toward their compound?

One big woman trudges to me
waiting to be nuzzled by my good hand.
She licks my palm
telling me of her stolen children,
her friends, her little ones
hauled away, never to be seen again
on these home pastures.

She knows
they've made meals
for many red-nosed, big bellied men
smiling hungry human kids
perhaps for other mothers, aunties,
grandmas, too.

She can't understand this forced giveaway.
She ruminates, always searching
she confides
for her calves, her little ones, her mate.

She has a few more seasons
but the memory of the brief visit
with that bull
fills her eyes with salt tears again.
He was not gentle with her
she remembers.

Cows have dreams of love, too
she told me.
Some chew their grass with relish
recalling as they calve
the creating of their children.
While others, pass the days getting fat
waiting till the time for slaughter.

They feel the branding.
They know it's only a matter of moons
before they will be carved up.

They have heard the moans before
the grasses in the wind warn them, trucks,
dogs and humans with horses
their executioners
will be coming once again.

(South Dakota)

THE NURSE UNDER THE BED

Written after reading an article about
Richard Speck

The terrible moment before he
left the room for the first time
when she
wasn't sure   he had counted her
seeing terror in the other seven
she wondered if
they hysterical might not
be the ones
to give her away.

Unseen force that helped her roll
with one breath
underneath the bed.
Absurd details now a comfort
the sloppy way she'd made the bed
oversize spread a protection suddenly
from his scan.

She prayed he'd keep the bright lights
turned off
grateful for her slight build
her ability to hold her breath

for minutes at a time.
She didn't dare look
at the faces of her friends
her colleagues
they might realize she'd hidden
might not be able to stifle
a scream   alert him
she keeps her eyes shut
as long as she can.

But, what might she do?
One by one, they are escorted
bound, gagged, muffled, murdered
in the next room.
She wasn't sure she wasn't dreaming
she hears screaming.
Her roommate's cry
the others in the room trying
to tear their bonds
but too late.

He enters again and takes them
by twos, his eyes betraying
his gentle voice
his eyes fired by his kills
she knows deep   the others
don't haveachance.

How long will he continue?
This agony of survival
helplessness, a hell without fire
the night,   the ushering in and out
the last dragged and disappeared
she holds her breath
listensfor   any   sound
hears breathing
and a door shut.
A door shut.

(New York City, USA)

FIRST ENCOUNTER WITH THE ILLUMINATI

Man is funereal
top hats, tail coats, faceless, stood up
in a pit of muddy ground
hands sheathed in black gloves
arms extending in mandible motions
mechanical scoopers opening
then closing ensemble giant metal digits
the hands, fingers, outreaching
above the terrain
in an unspoken ritual as rain begins
the drops on the ground in terminal
succession, swishing and anointing
long ebony limousines
lining up anonymously
opening like refrigerator doors
with a slight suction
before releasing their sinister occupants
under black umbrellas,
marching in battalions
to basso obscure organ music.

In the background, always
the threaten beckon
of my mother's voice.

They will shut me up, erase me.

I dash to shelter in an abandoned
half-light, green white, stone mansion.

Will angels protect me I wonder. Is God
almighty, powerful,
merciful to those who strive to travel
on the right path?

How can it be that children are allowed to
suffer so…?

(Toronto, Canada)

ERRATIC
WEATHERVANES   .3

Killing time's not what it's about
tap dance on grave stones if you must
but do a soft shoe.

Didn't you say it was a pity
about the earthquakes in Mexico?
All I remember was someone
fluffing pillows.

Sitting in the Planetarium on Sunday
eyes dome ward, waiting for the hush
the exit doors closed
we took in a breath.

Pulsars quavered
when the lights blew out
dramatic effects on a bowl shaped ceiling
designed to take our skepticism
away...hurrah.

After the show is over, I'm stiff
in the neck.
I cracked my back in both directions
but it didn't help.

Does it matter, you think
about the comet?

Conflicting reports about sum hurricane
coming down this way, they warned.
Is it we're supposed to batten
down the hatches
or open all those windows, I forget.

All that mimeo'd emergency advice
slides off my fingers
guess I'm a passive non-conformist
selectivity of impulse is the key.

Do the same when I take off in aircrafts
shut out the stewards pointing to their
shiny, white instruction sheets
yellow oxygen masks.

Laconic thoughts zip through me
in the PM.
I wait patiently for a bus on Sunday.
My mind was a total blank by noon,
anyhow.

Perhaps it will rain tomorrow
like they say.
When was it we anticipated dinner?
Yesterday...

We're damn lucky, I know to have
food down our tubes, but Christ,
it's creepy
I can still feel my own flesh and blood
but everywhere I look

All I see is shadows.

(New York City USA)

OGLALA FOREPLAY

You blow over me like El Nino
my heart becomes Montana
again the pulse of summer, rutting buffalo
sage seeds spraying, ripe choke cherries,
warm earth
lightning, recurring dreams,
pow wow drums.

We sit in darkness and sweat in a circle.
The wood we gathered together
burning the rocks.
Your voice deeper than the fire pit,
pleading in a sacred language, aloud
we ask for pity
breathing in the same thick, hot air.

You scoop me up, I'm six feet
above the ground,
furious, you hurl me down, shout at me
'Leave my land forever, give me your
clothes, walk home'

But when I try to go, you run after me
swishing your one braid in apology,
so we unclench our fists.

Why am I making you coffee, singing your
songs in the shower?

Why are we joking but not looking
at each other?
What are we daring, will you tell me,
kola...

(3 Mile Creek, Pine Ridge Reservation, South Dakota, USA)

FOR A.J.E.

With his tongue
engraving
on all my lips
his circular initials
curling his instrument,
that moistened
gentle muscle
rearing it's slippery head
and tickling then tasting
the damp
sweet walls within:

I am my own holiday
with Fourth of Julys
between my thighs
and Christmas
in my mouth.

(London, UK)

STATU$ETTES

Christmas trees with silver bulbs
(real silver?)
line the mirrored semi-halls
angles of clothing racks
on carpeted platforms
sitting/standing sales ladies
giving me not even the 'once over'
when they spy my army-navy
surplus jacket, last year's boots.

.

The women in the elevator
at Bergdorf Goodman's
have salt and pepper hair
they dyed white for chic.
They look peremptorily skyward
stroke their furs
with gold spangled fingers
nails too long for any menial tasks
wafting Estee Lauder and various Chanels
as they drift to the private collections
no matter what the season
their credit good decade round.

The women in the elevator at
Bergdorf-Goodman
shop at mid-morning, late afternoons
avoiding the tiresome lunchtime browsers
office carousers
plebeian window shoppers
who might prohibit their leisurely pace
their prime time view, their usual chair,
their usual 'girl'.
They keep their drivers waiting,
their limos
nudging buses, taxis and autos
to the back.

(New York City, USA)

WIRI WIRI

Flickering hands extend to you
back to my heart
from side to side, my words
my song, my head is numb.
My fingers sense the currents
of love between you and I.

Wiri wiri
my hair is turning gray
my waist no longer slim
my eyes no longer bright
my steps not light like yours.

But aie, wiri wiri
my hands will dance for you.
My arms would love to hold
your weathered face next to mine.

Ah, wiri wiri
weary, weary I am
of always saying, "goodbyes"
my tears will reach the ocean
before I see you again.

(Aotorea/New Zealand)

SOJOURNER IN THE MOJAVE

I should have known to be careful
in a summer of blue moons
and Saturn rings
I saw silver streaks on sandy pie-bald
mountain tops
a mirage clarified by highway perspective.

Propellers had been mounted
on aluminum stems
heralding the sun
spinning in random rhythms
to catch the breeze, like alien windmills
summoning Martians or maybe
Don Quixote.

Natural playgrounds of sandstone slides,
granite ladders, molded rocks
forming red-orange window ledges
where I saw a haunted Indian warrior
watching me.
He leaned against a monzonite ridge
while I smelled chalky wet rock splinters
in the waddies
letting the sun chisel lines
into my forehead
with his dry determined heat.

Silence surrounded me as a cool blanket
so quiet I held my breath at first
until an air force jet belched across the sky
tearing my ears with sound, with echoes.

Terrifying beauty at mid-day;
I fingered the seam of a boulder
fifty feet high
the crack occurring eons
before the scar appeared.
Quartz, mica, feldspar and iron
oozing with the rains
formed a living salve
spreading across the base
now rough and solid under my palms.

Visions in those Joshua trees
he was watching me
as we roamed Hidden Valley,
wandering where
we could find shade in a solitary
monument there
a placing of alkali flat breakers in a circle
we laid our clothes in lines
on the damp earth
creating a fire as we turned together
smoking signals to the blue patch above
until we swallowed slowly
slowly quenching our thirst
deep in the Mojave desert.

(Mojave Desert, California 1985)

IN LABOUR

Pinning purple washcloths on the line
the clouds suddenly change into prisms
sending pastel light around my face.
Soothing women's voices
in an unearthly chorus
swell into my ears and my baby, my baby
starts stretching again.

Dropping the clothes pegs,
I begin a slow dance
with my wee daughter.
A beatific smile inside us
as my nostrils open wider
smelling the summer breeze.

Powerful chords
resound through my back
cramping my watermelon stomach
Ooooo, Oh, I'd almost forgotten
this is how it begins, or is it the ending
of us, the-creating of 'she' and 'me'.

No more coherent English thoughts
as my body moves in her own lingo
I feel a herd of dolphins enter
hold my breath, French kissing the clouds
swimming through a forest at midnight
running the entire Atlantic ocean

before I open my eyes, exhale a long-aaah!

Rivulets ebb down my legs
my bare feet clench the grass
deep inside another clock commences.
There is time to finish hanging the
laundry, later.

(Hastings, New Zealand)

PRAYERS UNDER THE MOON

Oh moon, before you are full
take this sadness from me
transform it into moonlit tears
let loose from the sky in rains
soaking the earth,.

Oh, moon restore what's left
of my humanity.
Lift from me this weight of years
of faces, of places, of fears
shine down with your unearthly light
into my heart, so moon
I may plant seeds more gently
than those sown with hatred
or with blood.

(Kerhonkson, New York, USA)

COUNTRY COURTIN

In memory of time spent in Booligal

Leaning down, glass in hand, his eyes
expectant
he starts off with,
"Ya married?"
If I answer, "No"
He says
  "Right then."

If I respond, "Yes."
He continues,
"Happily?"
If I respond, "No"
He says
  "Right then."

If I answer, "Yes"
He goes on with
"He around?"
If I answer, "No"
He says
   "Right then."

If I respond, "Yes"
He persists.
"Ya ride horses?"

Either way I answer
He says
        "Right then."

(NSW, Australia)

LETTER TO DENALI ON K2

Oh Denali, if I could, I would go
to the ends of the earth to find you, to
cradle you once more.
I weep over the place where you fell- so
cruel that you are somewhere
on a mountain so near the sky, so far from
us mortals, that no one who loves you
could ever reach your place of death
on K-2.

If I could my son, I would go to that place
where you breathed your last breath,
freezing as it must have been, and warm
your bones.
Yet, even if I could go now, it is already
more than 50 days
since that avalanche swept you or you fell
trying to help your father.
Denali, you would no longer look like the
fine, healthy man you were
when you left for Pakistan.

Now nature has reclaimed you, Denali-
your skin must be blackened
with frost, your muscles twisted, bones
crushed, all your blood
run out of you or congealed

into the rocks and snow,
nothing left of your beautiful" guitar lake"
blue eyes
your hands no longer able to create,
to caress, to repair, to tie ropes
so expertly or plant flowers so patiently,
or paint so expressively, or pray, as you
did in so many places of prayer.

People will say many words to offer
consolation for your departure
from this earthly life.
But I am not consoled, my son.

Why did I not protect you enough? How
could I have done differently?   I want
God to answer me…there must
have been a way.
I cannot accept that you went gentle onto
that final pathway when everyone else
turned back except your mulish father.

This pain is sooo deep, deeper than the
400 foot scar the avalanche left widening
with every passing hour without you.
Denali- you must know –since you are
where you can hear me
hear all who silently cry, wordlessly
or copiously weep and scream at the fate
that took you from us, that stopped me
from stopping your father before he took
both your lives…too soon.

I don't want to say goodbye my son.
I do not feel you are gone from the
etheric realms we still co-exist in;
we interweave between thresholds.

My love extends to you across time,
across space, across death.
Until we meet again, Denali, may my
words and actions cheer your spirit, warm
you and, if necessary, right the wrongs
that have been done to you.

My motherhood never ceases.   You are
my son, Denali
no matter where you are
no matter what happened to you
no matter how much time has passed
since I last held you, ruffled your fine
head of hair and kissed you "goodbye".

Goodbye. Goodbye.

With waves of grief in an infinite sea
of memory
we try to say, yet I cannot bear to say…
goodbye.

(Riyadh, Saudi Arabia)

HE'LL WATCH THE STARS, YOU"LL WASH THE FLOORS
A Warning to Anyone who wants to marry a mountain guide

Now you gaze on equal ground, my dear
his eyes so undivided;
but soon his other love will make
demands
to be requited.

No matter what your charms, his arms
must wrap around another.
Your smooth young skin cannot compare
with limestone, granite, alpine air;
your legs, your lips, your rounded hips
may remind him of his mother.

Ah, you may climb together now
watch eagles soar below,
caress the rocks, bathe in the lakes
hear summit winds a blow.
But even if his buddy you be
be on guard when baby comes.
The vertical heights will call him more
to be 'provider' for his sons.

Then, traveling as a three some
with a teething, curious, child
will cramp his style, restrain his feet
and he'll howl for the wilds.

And you will, too, on those late nights
while feeding at your breast
is a beautiful, helpless, little one
who loves you most and best.
The glimmer in your eyes will shift
and the glimmer in his, too.

You and baby on the horizontal plane,
father in the sky so blue.

Lure of the heights, the snow, the rush
will rope your love away.
Then you and little "juniors"
will lonely pass each day.
All the while envisioning, thinking
of where he will be when,
then he comes home to hugs and tears
and flash---------he's off again.

There he'll be tying in, my dear
as you are in tied down,
he is ever heavenward
as you're submerged earthbound.

And he'll be watching the stars, my dear
as you'll be washing the floors,
and he'll be breathing the crisp, clear air

as you change the nappies once more.

He'll be carrying his pack and gear
as you haul the laundry baskets;
and your former life, lovers and dreams
drift away as you become wretched.

Then he'll be watching the clouds,
my dear
and you the calendar.
And he'll tell you 'never to fear', my dear
as you pray for him 'never to fall';
and he'll promise the moon and the sun
to you
but don't expect <u>him</u> at all.

Where he'll be rubbing his hands on ice
you'll be drying your children's' tears,
and you'll speak over radio and telephone
and your youth will pass with the years.

Don't expect that he'll bring you
the money.
No, you'll never see much my dear.

All the cash that he earns from his clients
will go to tickets, girlfriends and gear.
You'll never quite know his income
cause he'll stash it in foreign banks
yet if he buys you an ironing board
he'll sulk if you don't give him 'thanks'.

He'll be brimming with stories
and sights, my dear
though never a crag will you see,
but if you try to demand your share
he will burst the "shackles" free.

Then off to his mountain mistresses
to console him in his plight,
as you comfort your children in sickness
too tired now to fight.

And he'll moan
you've no sense of adventure
too steady for him as a match
and you'll fantasize him falling
emerging with only a scratch,
which somehow or other gets septic
and they must amputate his limb,
then climbing will be out of the question
and you'll finally be with him.

But no, he's discovered a new sport
one-legged skiing on vertical slopes.

So with a sigh and a shrug
you send your man off
for him there is no hope.

So take this as a warning
to all you climbing mates...
A mountain guide
may seem fun and wild,

But oh!
How he'll make you wait

(Bundilla, NSW, Australia)

SPOILS OF WAR

Early in the morning children wash their
faces in freezing street puddles
dust never settles on Kabul streets.
Drivers strain their eyes, their ears
for signs of trouble
no chit chat- just go, go, go, swerve
stop and go fast
Breathing returns to conflict zone normal
only after we are inside the checkpoints
then out of the vehicle.

Violence surrounds us
outside the perimeter
factions forever eroticizing hatred, stirring
sensations in their loins
connected with anger, bloodlust, revenge,
cruelty, pain.

Inside temporary shelters
fleeting feelings of security, relief
I dodge the ammo belts, stripper clips,
boxes of bullets.
We keep poker faces and hands
to our sides conscious of cameras, screens
eyes in the walls, in the skies.

Everyone here is a CHU prisoner
yearning to break free.

Vodka is served to steady nerves
at all times of the day
afternoon, evening, Fridays, holidays-
haram or not-this liquid is there.
Doesn't matter it becomes the medicine
for all ailments, body and soul
longing, memories are unleashed as the
alcohol pours into eager mouths
loosening tongues, spilling secrets,
staining reputations.

All by design, these games, trades,
profiling for the future, shot by shot.

Fatigue fades, fantasy invades, guards
change their posts, huddle
everywhere, even here, especially here-
people crave affection
brushing shoulders standing in lines,
hands lingering as they open doors
offer food, inspect your documents
take your bags for you.

The code of conduct toward western
women is unwritten yet known by all.

The risk here, the stakes are so high
most repress their desires, stifle
their faculties for thinking, their capacities
for loving by submerging themselves
in duties, in sleep, in drink
or in prayer.

Kabul may be the hub of the world for
adventure junkies.
Tactical or Joint operations centers of
nations united based in the capital
seethe with tension, combat anticipation
and/or the possibility of sexual favors,
gifted packages, fresh meat or forced
services from those too poor to object,
but too beautiful to escape attention.

(Kabul, Afghanistan)

AMBUSH

Wearing the cloak of religion to hide
the dagger of globalization
the spectre wheezes coughing up
the blood of bigotry.

Its hooded form concealing
rabbit red eyes,
sharpened sharks teeth, it creeps
like an epidemic infecting hearts,
sickening spirits, weakening the will
the scimitar of materialism
slashing anywhere it smells love.

A veil descends like an invisible chador
covering us in long, dark robes of despair.
We bow our heads against
the sandstorms of grief to come.

The sun is crying, oceans scream,
children refuse to be born.
Drums beat relentlessly, birds cease
building nests.
Mothers for the first time
must send their daughters
as well as their sons
off to war.

Nightmares deafen our sleep.

A muezzin blows his horn
suddenly..."Enough."
"Stop."
This sound implores us to listen.
He keens these words.
"There is not enough poverty
in the world."

The spectre demon twists,
contorting with delight and disbelief.

"No, we do not have enough poverty.
Poverty of prejudice,
poverty of ignorance,
poverty of oppression,
poverty of wrath, poverty of violence,
poverty of alienation, poverty of hate."

The demon halts just long enough
to allow
a newborn to laugh
little children to skip,
parents to embrace each other,
elders to feel the sun,
those in their sickbeds to breathe
without pain,
those about to commit crimes to forget
their evil intentions,
those about to run away

instead to turn and smile.

The muezzin is joined by rabbis,
monks, priests,
clever men and women,
by shaman, by acolytes, by nuns,
by angels.

This multitude is an army.
The spectre is surrounded.
They foil the menacing demon
with their silent unity

Peace.

(Wellington, New Zealand)